Love's LITTLE Recipes FOR Friendship

by Linda Shepherd

MULTNOMAH BOOKS SISTERS, OREGON

LOVE'S LITTLE RECIPES FOR FRIENDSHIP
published by Multnomah Books
a part of the Questar publishing family

© 1997 by Linda Shepherd

International Standard Book Number:1-57673-095-6

Cover design by Susan Luckey Higdon

Printed in the United States of America

Most Scripture quotations are from the *New International Version*
© 1973, 1984 by International Bible Society
used by permission of Zondervan Publishing House
Also quoted:
The King James Version (KJV)

For information:
QUESTAR PUBLISHERS, INC.
POST OFFICE BOX 1720
SISTERS, OREGON 97759
Library of Congress Cataloging-in-Publication Data:
Shepherd, Linda E., 1957–
    Love's little recipes for friendship/Linda Shepherd.
        p.cm.
    Cover title: Recipes for friendship.
    ISBN 1-57673-095-6 (alk. paper)
    1. Friendship—Religious aspects—Christianity. 2. Interpersonal
relations—Religious aspects—Christianity. 3. Love—Religious aspects—Christianity.
4. Friendship—Quotations, maxims, etc. 5. Love—Quotations, maxims, etc.
I. Title. II. Title: Recipes for friendship
BV4647.F7S54 1997
241'.6762—dc21   96-52138
                                                              CIP
97 98 99 00 01 02 03 04 05 06 — 10 9 8 7 6 5 4 3 2 1

*T*able of Contents

Friendship happens when
two hearts carry the same weight.

L.E.S.

I want to thank all the friends God has put into my life—
especially Debbie, Karen and Sharon.
A special thanks to my friend Marlee Alex
who spent many hours editing this book.
And I can't forget Marcia
who encouraged me with herbal tea and laughter
when I told her I would never write again.
Okay, you were right, Marcia! Now stop looking sooo smug!
Also, a special thanks to my prayer team!
God bless you all!

Linda

$\mathcal{I}$ntroduction

Many people do not know how to prepare friends properly. Instead of mixing friends with love, they put them in a jam, crush, snip or shred them.

Love's Little Recipes for Friendship will show you how to preserve lasting friendships as well as sweeten them with celebrations and spice with fun. You'll discover gourmet recipes for blending hellos and good-byes with sweet'n sour memories. You'll find professional hints from world-class chefs on how to desert bitterness and create nutritious spiritual main dishes. Don't forget the appetizer: friendship with God.

It is my hope that you and your friends will enjoy warm and delicious relationships for many years to come. Blessings!

Linda E. Shepherd

Friendship

Oh,
The comfort—
The inexpressible comfort
Of feeling safe with a person,
Having neither to weigh thoughts,
Nor measure words, but pouring them all right
out, just as they are, chaff and grain together,
Certain that a faithful hand will take and sift
them, keep what is worth keeping—
And with a breath of kindness,
Blow the rest
away.

Dinah Marie Mulock Craik, English Novelist, 1826-1887

Part One

ঌ

Garden Fresh Ingredients

Two are better than one,
because they have a good return for their work:
If one falls down, his friend can help him up.
But pity the man who falls and has no one to help him.

Ecclesiastes 4:9-10

Chapter One

❧

Lettuce Love

The best portion of a good man's life is his little, nameless, unremembered acts of kindness and love.

William Wadsworth, American Poet

A Special Mixture

Friendship is a special mix:
One smile of cheer,
A listening ear,
One hand to hold,
A love that's bold,
No knead for dough,
Just knead to know—
'Til my life's end—
You are my friend.
L.E.S.

Friendship Salad

Cook's Note: Toss the salad, not your friend. Keep your heart filled with love and your friendship will never wilt.

Ingredients:

Pear of friends
Lettuce enjoy one another
Mince words of anger
Pepper with love

Salt with conversation
Egg her on to reach her hard-boiled dreams
Sprouts of giggles
Nutty slivers of humor

Directions:
Toss and enjoy.
L.E.S.

*L*ove Never Fails

If I speak in the tongues of men and of angels,
but have not love,
I am only a resounding gong or a clanging cymbal.
If I have the gift of prophecy and can fathom all mysteries and all knowledge,
and if I have a faith that can move mountains,
but have not love,
I am nothing.
If I give all I possess to the poor and surrender my body to the flames,
but have not love,
I gain nothing.
Love is patient, love is kind.
It does not envy, it does not boast, it is not proud.
It is not rude, it is not self-seeking,
it is not easily angered, it keeps no record of wrongs.
Love does not delight in evil but rejoices with the truth.
It always protects, always trusts, always hopes, always perseveres.
Love never fails.

1 Corinthians 13:1-8

How to Choose a Good Friend

Selecting friends is much like selecting apples. Many friends are good on both the outside and the inside; others look good on the outside but are rotten at the core. Avoid bad friends like bad apples, lest you become one yourself.

To determine the character of an apple, you must peel it to see if its core is pure and good. To determine the character of a friend, you must also look into her heart. The heart of a good friend will be full of caring thoughts and loving attitudes. As you grow closer, the flavor of her life will be enhanced with your own. Together, your friendship will be a sweet fruit compote.

L.E.S.

The rotten apple spoils his companion.

Benjamin Franklin, American Philosopher and Statesman

He who walks with the wise grows wise, but a companion of fools suffers harm.

Proverbs 13:20

Who you love tells me who you are.

Folk Proverb

Ebbs of Love

Love is like a pure, clear pool
  Reflecting peaks and sky.
Bubbling life from mountains cool—
  A forest lullaby.
Loosed in silver ribbons fair
  It flows to ocean's floor.
Love is deep and stronger there.
  Than ever was before.
Though waves toss the salty sea,
  With winds that don't relent,
Love stays hidden, flowing free
  Beneath, in cool currents.

L.E.S.

Love is the fairest flower that blooms in God's garden.

Anonymous

Love covers all, like a fog resting over mountain and valley.

Folk Proverb

Chapter Two

ॐ

Relish Words

A kind word is better than a big pie.

Russian Proverb

*R*ecipe to Sweeten Someone's Day

Cook's Note: Serve not only to nice people; the unlovable need it most.

Ingredients:
1 pint cream of loving thoughts
1 pint affirmations
100 random acts of kindness
1 pound tact
100 leaves thyme

Directions:
Pour pint of cream of loving thoughts into your day. Do not skim(p)! Voice your thoughts into affirmations. Mix with tact and random acts of kindness. Blend together at the perfect thyme.

Warning: Avoid using sharp words; as you may have to eat them. Pride is most difficult to swallow, although it may reduce a big mouth.

L.E.S.

Nice words are free, so choose the ones which will speak well of you.

Folk Proverb

A kind word picks up a man when trouble lets him down.

Anonymous

Salt your conversation with kind words.

Folk Proverb

$\mathscr{G}$ood Conversation: A Piece of Cake

Cook's Note: The art of conversation is saying the right thing at the right time and avoiding the wrong thing and the wrong time, no matter how tempting.

Ingredients:

Set of ears for each person
2 or more voices
1 bushel ideas
1 pint curiosity
1 gallon questions

Directions:

Open all pairs of ears, but use only one voice at a time. To keep eyes from glazing, let each voice alternately add ideas to mix. Sift in curiosity and stirring questions. Bake 365 days a year. Serve generous portions to everyone you meet.

L.E.S.

$\mathcal{M}$ ississippi Mud Cake

Cook's Note: At your next tea party serve this rich mud cake instead of gossip. (*Gossip is unsanitary because you have to dirty your hands to sling mud.*)

Ingredients:

2 cups sugar
1 cup shortening
4 eggs
1 1/2 cup flour
1/4 teaspoon salt
1 teaspoon baking powder

1/3 cup cocoa
2 teaspoons vanilla
1 cup chopped pecans
1 large bag small marshmallows
Frosting (recipe follows)

Directions:

Cream sugar and shortening. Add eggs one at a time, beating well after each is added. Sift flour, cocoa, baking powder, and salt and add to mixture, mixing well. Mix in vanilla and pecans. Bake in greased and floured 9 x 13 inch pan 30 to 40 minutes at 350°. Remove from oven and spread a large bag of miniature marshmallows on top while still hot. Immediately spread with frosting.

Frosting:

1 stick margarine
1/3 cup cocoa
1 box powdered sugar

1/2 cup evaporated milk
1 teaspoon vanilla
1 cup chopped pecans

Directions:

Sift cocoa and sugar. Add melted margarine, milk, vanilla, and nuts. Mix well.

Chapter Three

ટ&

Fruity Fun

To double your fun, split it with a friend.

L.E.S.

Recipe for Friendship Ambrosia

Ingredients:

1 dozen friends
1 small can crushed ire
4 cups shredded coconut
1 dozen oranges
2 large cans crushed pineapple (undrained)
1 cup sugar
1 dozen cherries

Directions:

Bring your friends together and do not cut into pieces. Chill ire. Peel oranges, section and cut into small pieces. Stir together with coconut, pineapple and sugar. Spoon into dessert dishes and top with cherries. Serve to your friends with a listening ear and a tall glass of iced tea. Enjoy!

L.E.S.

*M*enu for Fun

Cook's Note: *For a good time, spread a buffet table with these:*

Ingredients:
Gathered nuts
Party paté
Sprouts of friendship
Loaves of laughs
Stuffed giggles garnished with guffaws
Raisin hopes pie

L.E.S.

Happiness sneaks in through a door you didn't know you left open.
John Barrymore, American Actor

Make two grins grow where there was only a grouch before.
Elbert Hubbard, American Editor and Lecturer, Pig-Pen Pete

A day is lost if one has not laughed.
French Proverb

*H*ow to Be the Life of the Party

Cook's Note: Caution. Never be angry at your friends for even a minute because you will lose sixty seconds of happiness.

Ingredients:
58 giggles
1 quart of grins
4 tablespoons gingered jests
1/2 cup grated sarcasm
1 ounce good manners

Directions:
Mix giggles into the punch to give smiles of fun. Refrain from grilling your companions with strong opinions and avoid eating too much garlic. Split your grins with others. Serve gingered jests that will cost neither friend nor foe. Carefully grate sarcasm, then toss the impulse to speak it. Stir all ingredients carefully with good manners and you will be invited to many more parties to come.

L.E.S.

How to Bake a Special Occasion Cake with Your Child

Remove 18 blocks and 7 toy cars from kitchen table. Heat oven. Have child get out bowls, spoons and ingredients. Have child grease pan while you crack nuts.

Measure out 2 cups of flour; remove child's hands from flour.

Put flour, baking powder and salt in sifter. Get dustpan and sweep up pieces of bowl that child knocked off the table. Wash child. Get another bowl. Answer doorbell.

Return to kitchen. Remove 1/2 inch salt from greased pan. Crack eggs into bowl. Answer phone.

Return to kitchen and find child. Brush flour and wash shortening off him. Take up greased pan and remove 1/2-inch layer of flour. Pick up nutshells from floor. Send child outside to play.

Wash kitchen floor. Wash table. Wash walls. Wash dishes. Call the baker. Lie down.

Author Unknown

Recipe for Celebration

Ingredients:

An occasion
A piece of your heart
Happiness
Guests to serve
Cake, cookies, punch (optional)

Directions:

The place to celebrate is here. The time to celebrate is now. Share your happiness by telling your friends your good news and invite them to a party. When friends arrive, serve them your heart. (Save a piece of your mind for later.) A good time will be shared by all.

L.E.S.

Laugh and grow strong.

St. Iqnatius of Loyola, Spanish Religious Leader

Want to be invited back? Always tell people a little less than they want to know.

L.E.S.

If an elephant invites you to his house, don't talk about his nose.

Folk Proverb

Jokes are the cayenne of conversation and the salt of life.

Paul Chatfield, English Writer and Parodist

If you can't remember a joke, don't dismember it.

Anonymous

*R*ecipe for Sourdough Fun

Cook's Note: Every friendship should create this recipe for fun.

Ingredients:
A bunch of good times
2 or more good eggs
3 cups titters and twitters
5 hoots of hilarity
Strains of great music
1 (or more) Un-bored game
Bubbles of laughter

Directions:
Pick good times as often as possible so they never spoil. Take good eggs and crack them up with yokes. Mix with titters, twitters and hilarity. Add to great music and games. This will help soured, doughy faces rise in bubbles of laughter.

L.E.S.

Laughter is one of the best things that God has given us, and with hearty laughter neither malice nor indecency can exist.

Stanley Baldwin, English Statesman and Writer

Part Two

ॐ

Preserving Good Things

"Love your neighbor as yourself."

Leviticus 19:18

Chapter Four

Good-Neighbor Marmalade

If a man is worth knowing at all, he is worth knowing well.

Alexander Smith, Scottish Poet, *Dreamthorp*

*H*ow to Treat a Neighbor

Cook's Note: *It would be easy to love the world if it weren't for the miserable woman who lives next door. Yet, no matter how miserable, treat her with love.*

Ingredients:
1 neighborhood barbecue
Barbecue Brisket (see next page)

Directions:
To make sure your neighbor is well done, treat her to a barbecue! Just be sure she is not the main course. It is important not to grill her, though you may toast her. Season with warm thoughts to help preserve the friendship.

L.E.S.

Good neighbors hold their heads up when they greet each other,
only they keep their noses at a friendly level.

Unknown

*B*est Oven-Barbecued Brisket

Cook's Note: Start a day or two before to make the best barbecue ever tasted!

Ingredients:

5-6 pounds brisket (or a 3-4 pound
   eye of round roast)
1 bottle liquid smoke
Garlic salt
Onion salt
Seasoned salt

1 tablespoon flour
1 oven bag
1 bottle barbecue sauce
   (onion flavored)
1/2 cup mild picante sauce

Directions:

Trim fat from brisket. Soak brisket all night in 1 bottle of liquid smoke. The next day, season meat with garlic, onion and seasoned salt. Put flour in oven bag and shake. Place meat and liquid smoke in flour-coated bag. Put bag into 2-inch deep baking dish. Place dish in 400° oven for approximately 15 minutes. Reduce heat to 200° and cook 10 to 12 hours. Allow meat to cool in its own juice.

Drain juice and boil until thick. Add barbecue sauce and picante sauce and simmer.

Slice brisket. Place in a foil-lined pan and pour barbecue sauce over sliced meat. Heat at about 200° for one hour.

*G*ood-Neighbor Shake

Cook's Note: *This shake will help melt icy hearts.*

Ingredients:

1 pair open eyes	A moment's time
1/4 cup courtesy	2 cups chat
Plenty of cooperation	52 weeks plain-vanilla days

Directions:

Start by opening your eyes to your own faults. Pick up your yard and turn down your stereo. (Most neighbors want to enjoy their own music, not yours.)

Next, use your blender to frappe 1/4 cup courtesy with cooperation for several moments. Add vanilla days and blend until smooth. Pour this refreshing drink into two cups chat. (Too much chat could turn you into a nuisance.) Drink a cup of this mixture weekly, and you will see your neighbor turn into a friend right before your eyes.

L.E.S.

If you have an unpleasant neighbor, the odds are that he does, too.

Anonymous

How to Return a Borrowed Cup of Coffee

Cook's Note: *The best thing to borrow from your neighbor is her good humor. Yet it may dissolve if you don't return her invitations. Invite her to share a cup of coffee at your house.*

Ingredients:
3/4 cup ground coffee
3 cups water
Flavoring (your choice)
4 teaspoons sugar (optional)
1 cup whipped cream (optional)

Directions:
Brew coffee and water in your coffee maker. Pour steaming into mugs. Add drops of flavoring and 1 to 2 teaspoons of granulated sugar to each cup. Top with whipped cream and serve immediately.

L.E.S.

Lend to a friend only if you are willing to lose the money, otherwise you will gain an enemy.

Folk Proverb

Neither a Borrower nor a Lender Be:
For loan oft loses both itself and friend,
And borrowing dulls the edge of husbandry.

Shakespeare, English Poet and Dramatist, *Hamlet*

A rare volume is a borrowed book that comes back.

Anonymous

Love your enemies. After all, they never borrow from you.

Unknown

Top Ten Good Deeds to Give Your Neighbor

Cook's Note: The kindness you spread today will be returned tomorrow.

1. Pick up your neighbor with a kind word.
2. When you drop your kids off at school, drop off your neighbor's, too.
3. Helping with yardwork is a kindness that covers more beautifully than a blanket of fresh snow.
4. Entertain your neighbors when you entertain your friends.
5. Bury grudges (see recipe in later chapter).
6. When calamity strikes your neighbor and you don't know what to say, say a prayer.
7. Let your neighbor's children play at your house.
8. Give the gift of hospitality; invite your neighbor over for a visit.
9. In times of trouble, take a meal to your neighbor.
10. Never expect payment or borrowed items to return.

L.E.S.

You will never get dizzy when doing a good turn, even though one good turn deserves another.

L.E.S.

Chapter Five

৯৯

Long-Distance Preserves

Distance can never untie the strings of friendship.

L.E.S.

*C*aramel Popcorn Treat to Mail

Cook's Note: *If you can't pop in to see your long-distance friend,*
pour this recipe into a decorative tin. Send in your place.

Ingredients:

3 quarts popped popcorn
1/2 cup white Karo syrup
1/4 teaspoon cream of tartar

1 cup brown sugar
1 stick margarine
1 teaspoon baking soda

Directions:

Pop popcorn and pour into large brown paper bag. Next, put brown sugar, Karo syrup, margarine and cream of tartar in microwave safe bowl. Heat mixture in microwave 45 seconds to 1 minute. Stir. Heat for another minute or until boiling. Stir in baking soda. (Don't forget this). Pour caramel over popped corn in bag and mix well. Fold top of bag and place in microwave. Cook on high 1 minute. Remove bag and shake well. Repeat process until corn is golden brown. Pour onto large cookie sheets to cool.

Sweets to the sweet: farewell!

William Shakespeare, English Poet and Dramatist, *Hamlet*

*R*ecipe to Bridge the Miles

Ingredients:

1 mountain of stationery

1 or more photos (optional)

1 wad currency

1 book stamps

12 colossal phone bills

Directions:

To keep a long-distance friend, connect the dots between two lonely hearts. Fill stationery with creamed words:

Dear _____:

I was thinking of you today and wanting to write you a note. I miss you so much and wish you could be here to share a cup of tea with me. Instead, let us share this letter.

Here is the latest thing that's happened: (Insert story here.)

You won't believe this! (Insert story here.)

Just last night _____ was saying, (Insert quote here.)

So, how are you doing? Please write back and tell me what's new.

Your Friend,

_____

Fold letter and slide it into the envelope with optional photos. Wait two to three weeks for a response. If no response is sent, use same format to write a new letter.

If you grow impatient for a reply, pick up your phone and call. Then toss your phone bill with currency. For those online, send e-mail through the Internet to one another.

L.E.S.

If I had more time, I would write a shorter letter.

Blaise Pascal, French Philosopher and Mathematician

The cure for writer's block is writer's cramp.

Unknown

When you want a friend to call, make sure you're not sending busy signals. Keep plenty of friendly hellos on hand arranged with ringing conversation.

L.E.S.

My Friend

You have birthed in me a new world.
And now that you must go,
You take my world with you.
But oh,
Sweet memories bring it back to life!

L.E.S.

Chapter Six

৵

Homemade Hospitality

Friendship is a living thing that must be nourished.

L.E.S.

 **arm Welcomes**

Directions:

Slip an open door into a warm invitation. When guests arrive, invite them to dine on food for thought as you break bread together. Quench their thirst with tall glasses of fellowship.

L.E.S.

Better a meal of vegetables where there is love than a fattened calf with hatred.

Proverbs 15:17

You don't need money to entertain from your heart.

Folk Proverb

Tea Time Blessing

Lord, stir into our lives laughter and joy as we steep our friendship in your warmth.
May our friendship be strong so we may serve you together. Let us be scented with
the aroma of love as lumps of grief dissolve into our sweet camaraderie.

L.E.S.

Tea Time

Ingredients:
5 bags flavored tea
Teapot
Tea kettle
Milk
Lemon, honey or sugar to taste

Directions:
Heat fresh, cold water to boil in tea kettle. Warm teapot by rinsing it with hot water. Pour hot water into teapot and immerse tea bags. Steep for 5 minutes. Be sure to cover your teapot with a towel or tea cozy to keep it warm. Pour milk or lemon (optional) into china cups, add brewed tea and sweeten to taste.

L.E.S.

Tea Cakes

Ingredients:
1 cup margarine, softened
1/2 cup powered sugar
1 teaspoon almond extract
2 1/4 cup flour
Pinch of salt
3/4 cup flaked almonds

Directions:
Preheat oven to 400°. Cream butter, sugar and extract. Slowly add flour, salt and almonds. Blend till soft dough forms. Shape dough into 1-inch balls and place on ungreased baking sheet. Bake 10 to 12 minutes until set but not brown. Roll warm cookies in powered sugar. Cool. Roll again.

As the freshly poured tea settles into comfortable warmth, gentle conversation—so different from the frantic rush of everyday—opens the heart to new possibilities.

Emily Barnes, *If Teacups Could Talk*

Pumpkin Pie Quiche

*Cook's Note: Pull this nutritious, delicious quiche out of the oven
to serve to a friend for a lovely brunch.*

Ingredients and Directions:

Crust:

2 cups bread crumbs

2/3 cup oil

2 cups flour

Preheat oven to 400°. Mix bread crumbs, oil and flour. Press onto bottom and sides of two foil-lined cake pans.

Filling:

16 oz fresh or canned pumpkin

2 large sweet potatoes

1 cup leeks or onions, chopped

1 cup celery, chopped

4 eggs

1/2 cup milk

2 cups bread crumbs

1/4 teaspoon ground nutmeg

1/4 teaspoon red pepper

1/4 teaspoon pepper

1 teaspoon salt

1 cup flaked almonds

Peel and grate pumpkin and potatoes. Combine with remaining ingredients, except almonds. Mix well. Spoon mixture into crusts. Sprinkle pies with flaked almonds. Cover with foil. Bake 90 minutes. Remove foil and cook 10 more minutes until nuts are slightly brown. Delicious hot or cold.

Part Three

ಶ

Dishing Greetings

A smile is a friendly greeting in any language.

Unknown

Chapter Seven

୬ଲ

Appetizing Hellos

*A friend is like a mirror. The mood of your greeting
reflects on her face.*

L.E.S.

Make Time for Friends

Ingredients:
1 or more good ideas
2 tablespoons love
2 cups adventure
2 ounces memory-makers

Directions:
Melt shyness with love: Call or write your friend to say, "I'm glad we know each other. Let's do something together."

Whip in adventure and fold in colorful memory-makers.

L.E.S.

True riches comes not from golden coins but from golden friendships.

L.E.S.

If you want to get close to someone, try his diet.

Anonymous

New Neighbor Thing-a-Ma-Jigg Cookies

Cook's Note: Quick and easy goodies to bring to a new neighbor.

Ingredients:
2 cups sugar
1 stick butter or margarine
1/4 cup cocoa
1/2 cup milk
1/2 cup peanut butter
1 teaspoon vanilla
3 cups rolled oats

Directions:
In a 2- or 3-quart pan, bring sugar, butter, cocoa and milk to a boil, stirring constantly. Boil for one minute, continuing to stir. Remove pan from heat and add peanut butter and vanilla. With large spoon, stir until dissolved. Stir in rolled oats until well blended. Use teaspoon to drop warm cookie dough onto waxed paper.

After cookies have cooled, arrange several on a festive paper plate. Cover with plastic wrap and tie with bow. Bring plate to your new neighbor.

Makes approximately 50 to 60 cookies.

Chapter Eight

🐛

Slice of Good-Bye

I was moved to stay but life moved me anyway.

L.E.S.

$\mathcal{R}$ecipe for Moving Bag

Cook's Note: This is perfect for a friend who will be driving a long distance to her new home.

Ingredients:

1 large brown paper sack
Fresh water
1 empty pop container for each member of the family
Felt-tip markers
A handful of stickers
Construction paper
Stapler
Apples

Napkins
1 yard ribbon
Plastic sandwich bags
Travel Gorp (recipe follows)
Extra-large storage bag
1 package soft tortillas
1 can aerosol cheese spread
A handful of colorful pompoms

If children are traveling add:

1 set colored pencils for each (won't melt like crayons will)
Coloring books
Drawing pads

•Decorate the brown paper bag with stickers and markers.

•The night before, fill clean plastic pop bottles to 4 inches from the top with fresh water. Write the name of one traveler on each. Place in freezer overnight, and then into the brown paper bag the next day. The ice will melt and provide cool drinking water the next day.

•Stack several sheets of construction paper. Staple along the left edge to make a book. On the cover of the book write:

> *I'm your little moving bag,*
> *I want to tag along.*
> *Inside you'll find some great treats.—*
> *Our way to say, "So long!"*

On the inside pages, let friends and family decorate and write special messages to the traveling family.

•Put apples into the brown bag, along with napkins rolled together and tied with ribbon.

•Store Travel Gorp in freezer bags and place in the paper bag.

•Add soft tortillas and cheese spread to the paper sack.

• Put pompoms into sandwich bag. Slip this message inside:

I'm sending you some warm fuzzies to help unfray the moving blues. Use as needed.

Blue:	*I miss you, too.*
Pink:	*A blush of love.*
Red:	*Good wishes from our hearts.*
Green:	*Grow new friends.*
Black:	*Hope in your dark moments.*
Yellow:	*Sunshine wherever you go.*
White:	*Pure joy!*
Purple:	*Prayers for you.*

L.E.S.

Travel Gorp

Ingredients:
1 can mixed nuts
1 package M & Ms candies
1 small box Cheerios
1 bag miniature marshmallows

*S*ay Good-Bye

Say good-bye,
  but not forever.
Say good-bye,
  but come again.
Say good-bye,
  for parting never,
    ever comes between close friends.

L.E.S.

To part is always to die a little.

French Proverb

Chapter Nine

ॐ

Sweet'n Sour Memories

We must always have old memories and young hopes.

Arséne Houssaye, French Author

You are never alone when you are surrounded by warm memories.

L.E.S.

Do not squander time, for that is the stuff life is made of.

Benjamin Franklin, American Philosopher and Statesman

O memory, thou bitter sweet—both a joy and a scourge!

Mme. Anne Louise Germaine de Sta'l, French Novelist and Woman of Letters

 *ecipe for Jotting Memories*

Ingredients:
1 bottle brown tea ink (recipe follows)
1 fountain pen
1 blank volume, bound

Directions:
Dip your pen into ink and pause to refresh your memory. The following are suggestions that will help you get started:

1. What was the most interesting thing that happened today?

2. What made you laugh?

3. What special role did children play in your day?

4. Describe your most intimate conversation.

5. What made you cry?

Fill at least one page of your bound volume.

L.E.S.

We spend our years as a tale that is told.

Psalms 90:9 (KJV)

Recipe for Brown Tea Ink

Cook's Note: Steep your own brown ink so you can use it to journal the pages of your life.

Ingredients:
1/2 cup water
5 bags black tea

Directions:
Boil water and pour into teapot. Add tea and steep for 15 minutes. Stir vigorously. Strain tea leaves and cool. Pour into glass bottle.

Gather ye rose-buds while ye may,
Old Time is still aflying,
And this same flower that smiles today,
Tomorrow will be dying.

Robert Herrick, English Poet, *Hesperides*

How to Make a Memory Click

Cook's Note: Snap a few visual keepsakes to keep those memories alive.

Ingredients:
1 camera
1 or more rolls of film
1 or more photo albums
Construction paper
1 or more colored markers
Dozens of stickers
Scissors

Photo Shoot Tips:
1. Get close enough to fill your frame with heads and shoulders.
2. Never have your subjects squint into the sun. Keep the sun to the side.
3. Use the flash indoors and outdoors to soften shadows.
4. Don't line your subjects up against a wall; pose them in settings with scenic backgrounds, like near playground equipment.
5. Take several variations and angles of each shot.

Album Tips:

1. Use acid-free paper, which will not ruin photos.
2. Select and arrange photos in chronological order; cut into fun shapes.
3. Decorate album pages with stickers and brightly colored shapes of paper.
4. Glue photos onto decorated backgrounds.
5. Include page titles and captions for all photos.

L.E.S.

All to myself I think of you,
Think of the things we used to do,
Think of the things we used to say,
Think of each happy bygone day,
Sometimes I sigh, and sometimes I smile,
But I keep each olden, golden while
All to myself.

Wilbur D. Nesbit, *All to Myself*

Part Four

&

Heavenly Hashings

Then Jesus declared, "I am the bread of life. He who comes to me will never go hungry, and he who believes in me will never be thirsty."

John 6:35

Chapter Ten

Melting Hearts to God

Man warms his heart whenever he prays.

L.E.S.

*T*asty Turnovers

Cook's Note: *To find out how good God is, taste this:*

Take one pastry of life, filled with tears of sorrow that have been fried in hot oil. Turnover to God. Top with thanks. Tastes heavenly!

L.E.S.

Taste and see that the LORD is good; blessed is the man who takes refuge in him.

Psalm 34:8

*W*ho is God?

God is God.
Deuteronomy 7:9

God is mighty.
Job 36:5

God is holy.
Psalm 99:9

God is merciful and forgiving.
Daniel 9:9

God is light.
1 John 1:5

God is love.
1 John 4:8

Recipe for Becoming New

Cook's Note: *This recipe is the delight of the humble in spirit.*

Ingredients:
1 Bible
1 open heart
2 bended knees
1 humble spirit
1 invitation

Directions:
Open the Good Book and read John 3:16. Open your heart. If its hinges are stiff or rusty, pry it open on bended knees. With humble spirit, invite God to make you brand new.

L.E.S.

Seeker's Prayer

Oh Lord, it is hard to trust what I cannot see. It is difficult to reach for what I cannot yet grasp. Help me stretch my world to encompass truth so I may discover you.

L.E.S.

"You will know the truth, and the truth will set you free."

John 8:32

You cannot stay where you are and go with God.

L.E.S.

How to Move with God

Cook's Note: Begin with one step.

Ingredients:
The darkness of night
1 lamp

Directions:
Arise in the darkness of night. Trim your lamp with the Bible which will illuminate your path one step at a time.

Don't panic—you are not alone! Not only is God going to chart every step of your journey, he is going with you! Move with him.

L.E.S.

By perseverance the snail reached the ark.

Charles Spurgeon

God hasn't called me to be successful. He's called me to be faithful.

Mother Teresa

Fear not tomorrow, for God is already there.

Anonymous

Chapter Eleven

Blends of Blessings

Any concern too small to be turned into a prayer
is too small to be made into a burden.

Corrie ten Boom

How to Make Prayer Gravy

Cook's Note: *For best results, pour prayer on everything.*

Ingredients:

1/2 cup burdens
1 cup praise
1 cup concerns
1 pair of knees
1 pint thoughts and feelings
Teaspoon of God's comfort

Directions:

Pour drippings from your burdens into a bowl. Mix thoroughly with praise and let it rise to the top. Skim and set aside.

On stove top, blend your concerns and cook over low heat. Stir in praise, adding thoughts and feelings. Heat on high until prayers begin to bubble and a delicious aroma rises to heaven. Listen for God's quiet voice. Season with his comfort.

L.E.S.

Very early in the morning, while it was still dark, Jesus got up,
left the house and went off to a solitary place, where he prayed.

Mark 1:35

The Lord's Prayer

Our Father which art in heaven,
Hallowed be thy name.
Thy kingdom come.
Thy will be done in earth, as it is in heaven.
Give us this day our daily bread.
And forgive us our debts, as we forgive our debtors.
And lead us not into temptation, but deliver us from evil:
For thine is the kingdom, and the power, and the glory, for ever.
Amen.

Matthew 6:9-13 (KJV)

You must sink to your knees before you can rise to your feet.

L.E.S.

The trouble with being an atheist is you have nobody to talk to when you're alone.

Anonymous

Be joyful always; pray continually; give thanks in all circumstances,
for this is God's will for you in Christ Jesus.

1 Thessalonians 5:16-18

ℛecipe for a Rope of Prayer

Just as two or three strands of fiber can be woven into rope, so you and one or two friends can create a rope of prayer. Agree upon a request. Twist your requests together as you pray.

The more strands of prayer you twist together, the stronger your rope. **Caution:** *Though God delights in hearing from you, do not use your rope to lasso God into running your errands. Instead, use it to connect with the power of the sovereign Lord of the Universe.*

L.E.S.

"This is the confidence we have in approaching God:
that if we ask anything according to his will, he hears us."

1 John 4:14

*S*tormy Seas

Wind-swept waves washed through my boat
 And I could not foresee
How I could keep my ship afloat
 Upon this raging sea.

My storm-crossed life had come to this
 No one could save me now
All hope I had I now dismissed
 To face the wind's dark howl.

"Oh God," I prayed, "I can't go on
 Across this wind-roughed sea."
"My child," God said, "I'll bring the dawn
 When you cry out to me."

"Lord, save me then," I cried in kind.
 The sea lapped into peace.
Call out to God and you will find
 Your gale-tossed waves will cease.

L.E.S.

The sea of doubt is crossed by using oars of faith.

L.E.S.

Chapter Twelve

୬

Stirrings of Faith

Feed your faith and doubt will starve to death.

Anonymous

How to Make Spiritual Fruit

Cook's Note: *This recipe produces spiritual fruit in all seasons.*

Ingredients:
The Good Book
365 dates

Directions:
Set aside 365 dates, yearly. Cover tightly with prayer and chill the desire to sleep in. Arise early to study the Good Book and to have quiet talks with God.

L.E.S.

"Remain in me, and I will remain in you. No branch can bear fruit by itself; it must remain in the vine. Neither can you bear fruit unless you remain in me."

John 15:4

Each day speaks of God.

Folk Proverb

"If ye have faith as a grain of mustard seed, ye shall say unto this mountain, Remove hence to yonder place; and it shall remove; and nothing shall be impossible unto you."

Matthew 17:20 (KJV)

A Seed of Faith

A seed of faith, a flower pot,
Can be a very fragrant thought.
Unless you plant you can't assume
A lovely rose will ever bloom.

L.E.S.

Bloom where you are planted.

Unknown

The man who believes in nothing but himself lives in a very small world.

Anonymous

Faith never panics.

Unknown

Sorrow looks back, worry looks around, faith looks up.

Unknown

Faith is to believe what we do not see; and the reward of this faith is to see what we believe.

St. Augustine

Part Five

èa

Measuring Manners

Love covers over all wrongs.

Proverbs 10:12

Chapter Thirteen

ᨇ

Grating Gossip

The best thing to do behind a person's back is to pat it.

Anonymous

$\mathcal{S}$top Gossip Tea

Cook's Note: *Take care not to brew a strong sense of rumor with your tea.*

Ingredients:
1 serving of tea
Two or more people
One conversation
2 or more zipped lips

Directions:
Pour the tea. Engage in conversation, leaving out other people's business. If your friend offers a tidbit of gossip, politely refuse it. To keep from adding to any gossip spread before you, zip your own lips.

L.E.S.

A gossip separates close friends.

Proverbs 16:28

Conversation exercises the mind; gossip exercises the tongue.

L.E.S.

When three people are talking it is called conversation;
when one of them leaves, it is called gossip.

L.E.S.

The words of a gossip are like choice morsels; they go down to a man's inmost parts.

Proverbs 18:8

How to Keep a Secret

Cook's Note: Keeping a secret does not mean lowering your voice when you tell it, neither does it mean refusing to tell who told it to you. To keep a secret means to not tell.

Ingredients:
Cup of unspilled beans
Dash of forgetfulness

Directions:
Most people think secrets are a burden. They are anxious to share them because it helps to have someone carry them. The problem arises because this process usually continues, one person at a time, until the secret is public knowledge.

To keep your cup of unspilled beans, add a dash of forgetfulness so you will forget what you are told.

Use caution in sharing a secret of your own. After all, if you could not contain it, the person you tell may not be able to either.

L.E.S.

It's a great kindness to entrust people with a secret.
They feel so important while telling it to their friends.
Anonymous

Most folks can keep a secret; it's the folks they tell it to who can't.
Anonymous

None are so fond of secrets as those who do not mean to keep them.
Charles Caleb Colton, English Epigrammatist

Taming the Tongue

If you are having problems taming your tongue, try chewing a sprig of parsley or popping a mint in your mouth. Not only will this sweeten your breath, but it will keep you quiet because it is rude to talk when you are eating.

L.E.S.

> *"...take note of this: Everyone should be quick to listen,*
> *slow to speak and slow to become angry...."*
>
> James 1:19

Chapter Fourteen

Warming Rifts

The hardest thing to give is in.

Anonymous

*P*atch a Broken Friendship

Cook's Note: You can always patch a broken friendship.
The patch may show, but the friendship will be stronger than ever.

Directions:

To apply a patch to the tear in your friendship, use stitches of love with the thread of apology.

L.E.S.

There is so much good in the worst of us,
And so much bad in the best of us,
That it ill behooves any of us
To find fault with the rest of us.

Unknown

Hot Cross Buns

Cook's Note: This is a perfect peace-offering to your offended friend.

Ingredients:

2 packages dry yeast
3/4 cup lukewarm water
1/2 cup lukewarm milk
1/2 cup potato flakes
1/2 cup sugar
1 teaspoon salt
1/2 cup soft margarine
2 eggs

1/4 teaspoon nutmeg
1 teaspoon cinnamon
1 cup raisins
4 1/2 cups flour
1 egg yolk
2 tablespoons cold water

Directions:

Dissolve yeast in warm water. In mixing bowl, stir in milk, flakes, sugar, salt, margarine and eggs. Blend on low speed until smooth. Gradually add flour to form soft dough. Stir in nutmeg, cinnamon and raisins.

Knead dough on floured board for 5 minutes or until smooth and elastic. In warm place, let dough rise in greased, covered bowl until dough is doubled (about 1 1/2 hours).

Punch dough down. Cut into 32 pieces and shape into smooth balls. Place 2 inches apart on greased baking sheet.

With your kitchen scissors, snip a cross on top of each ball. Cover and let buns rise about 40 minutes or until doubled in size.

Heat oven to 375°. Brush top of buns with glaze of mixed egg yolk and cold water. Bake 20 minutes or until golden brown. Frost with icing.

Icing:
1 cup powered sugar
1 tablespoon milk
1/2 teaspoon vanilla

Mix until smooth. Spread on hot cross buns.

Three of the most difficult yet healing words to speak are, "Please forgive me."

L.E.S.

How to Bury Your Grudges

Cook's Note: If you are tempted to find fault with your neighbor, stop and count ten faults of your own.

If you happen to unearth someone's faults, bury your impulse to criticize, but not with a series of little digs.

Fertilize faults with forgiveness so you can look across the back fence and smile at your neighbor.

L.E.S.

Keep cool; anger is not an argument.

Daniel Webster, American Statesman

*Then Peter came to Jesus and asked, "Lord, how many times shall I forgive
my brother when he sins against me? Up to seven times?"
Jesus answered, "I tell you, not seven times, but seventy-seven times."*

Matthew 18:21-35

To err is human, to forgive, divine.

Alexander Pope, English Poet and Critic

Forgiveness is the fragrance the violet sheds on the heel that has crushed it.

Mark Twain, American Humorist

Chapter Fifteen

ಎ

Deserting Rudeness

The best seasoning is the salt of patience.

Folk Proverb

*R*ecipe for Canning Courtesy

Ingredients:
1/2 cup thank yous
1 pint pleases
1 quart patience
Sugared smiles to taste

Directions:
Place thank yous in sauce pan with pleases. Bring slowly to a boil, adding patience gradually. Simmer. Remove from heat, add smiles and stir. Pack courtesy into jars of joy processed in boiling water bath for 10 minutes. Makes 2 quarts. L.E.S.

Life is not so short but that there is always time enough for courtesy.
Ralph Waldo Emerson, American Philosopher and Essayist

Thanks is free to give.
Folk Proverb

Manners are the happy ways of doing things.
Ralph Waldo Emerson, American Philosopher and Essayist

*R*ecipe *for a Listening Ear*

Cook's Note: *Some friends give you their full attention without hearing a word you say. Don't make this mistake. Listening is a lasting gift. Give to everyone.*

Ingredients:

1 friend	Sprinkles of nods
2 ears	Loads of "hmmms" or grunts
1 mouth	of acknowledgment
1 banana	2 wide eyes

Directions:

To use your ears, you must shut your mouth. If your mouth won't shut, insert a ripe banana. Chew banana slowly or not at all. This will give your ears a chance to hear something other than the sound of your own voice.

As you listen, sprinkle your friend with nods, adding "hmmms" at will. If you are not nodding or humming, your friend may feel compelled to repeat herself. If this should happen, widen your eyes and add occasional grunts of acknowledgment. Even if you never say a word, your friend may feel you are the greatest conversationalist in the world.

L.E.S.

*R*ecipe for Tact

Take turns
Ask first
Converse courteously
Thank others

L.E.S.

Disagree without being disagreeable.

Unknown

A moral, sensible, and well-bred man
Will not affront me, no other can.

William Cowper, English Poet

*S*even Ways to Fray Your Neighbor's Nerves

Cook's Note: Caution: this dish causes indigestion and should be avoided.

Directions:
1. Buy things your neighbor can't afford. It will keep her in debt.
2. Throw a party and don't invite her, then play your music as loudly as you can until one in the morning.
3. Allow your children and pets to play in her yard.
4. Buy your husband a power saw.
5. Try to steal a few minutes of your neighbor's time several times a day.
6. Never return what you borrowed.
7. Argue with your windows open.

L.E.S.

You don't have to be an accomplished musician to play on your neighbor's nerves.

Anonymous

Politeness Prayer

Lord please tutor me to be
A friendly face to those I see.
And let me act with courtesy
When others do bump into me.

L.E.S.

Love one another deeply from the heart.

1 Peter 1:22

Notes:

Grateful acknowledgment is made to the authors and publishers for the use of the following material. Every effort has been made to contact original sources. If notified, I will be pleased to rectify any omissions in future editions.

Permissions and Sources:

Selected quotes referenced as Anonymous, from *14,000 Quips & Quotes For Speakers, Writers, Editors, Preachers, and Teachers,* compiled by E. C. McKenzie, ©1980 Baker House Book Company. Used by permission.

How to Bake a Special Occasion Cake with Your Child, Author Unknown, *With Love...and a Pinch of Salt,* Jessie Rice Sandberg, 1977, Sword of the Lord Publishers.

Linda Shepherd can be reached via email at: Lswrites@aol.com